About Pets **editorial team**

Parakeets
Budgerigars

Buying, nutrition, housing, behavior,
reproduction, health and lots more

Contents

Foreword

This book has been written by a devotee for devotees. We want to pass on to you the experience gained in more than 40 years of keeping and breeding birds. This book is for those who want to keep one or more budgerigars as a pet and who may one day want to breed them.

This book does not claim to provide a complete survey of budgie keeping but is intended to teach you the rudiments, and thus point the way towards becoming a budgie fan. For specialist information we draw your attention to publications by The Budgerigar Society.

We would like to thank those fans whose birds we were allowed to photograph at exhibitions and the breeders who permitted us to take photographs in their homes.

Your *About Pets* editorial team

ibooks

Distributed by Simon & Schuster, Inc.
1230 Avenue of the Americas,
New York, NY 10020

ibooks, inc.
24 West 25th Street
New York, NY 10010

The ibooks World Wide Web Site
Address is:
http://www.ibooks.net

ISBN 0-7434-4529-5
First ibooks, inc. printing
November 2002
10 9 8 7 6 5 4 3 2 1

Senior Consultant Lisa K. Allen, DVM
Cover photograph
copyright © 2002
Welzo Media Productions
Cover design by j. vita

As the purchaser of this book, you are
entitled to access a free electronic book
version of the title for use with
Windows, Macintosh and Palm
computers and PDAs. To access the
"ebook" version, you may log onto
www.ibooks.net, click the "about pets"
button and follow the directions.

Original title: *de Grasparkiet*

© 2002 Welzo Media Productions bv,

Warffum, the Netherlands

http://www.overdieren.nl

Photos:

Rob Doolaard, Piet Onderdelinden,

Europet en Rob Dekker

Printed in China

In general

The budgerigar is one of the most popular types of parakeet in the world. The Englishman Shaw was the person who first described this bird and gave it a name.

He gave it the English name "undulated parakeet" and, as a Latin name, *psittacus undulatus.* This means a parakeet with wavy markings. Later, the famous English ornithologist John Gold changed the Latin name to *melopsittacus undulatus.* In English, this type of parakeet is called "budgerigar," and its German name is *Wellensittich.*

Origins
The budgie is found almost every-where in Australia. Its territory extends over almost the entire interior of the continent; it is only not found in coastal areas. It is a bird from the red heart of Australia, which owes its name to the red color of the ground and the rocks there. In this region, the budgie leads a roving existence once the

brooding season is over. It flies about in search of areas with enough food and, above all, water. Water is vital for every living being and budgies can therefore most often be found in regions with watering places. Several times a day, early in the morning

and before sunset, sometimes in flocks of several thousand birds, they look for places where water can be found. If there is no more water to be found in a particular region, they move on to another region. Food is more readily available. The interior of Australia is an area where there are not many trees but where the wide expanses are covered with low shrubs and many sorts of grass. Even dried-up grass is food for these birds. They eat grass from the stalks or find the blades on the ground.

Buying a budgerigar

If you are thinking of buying one or more budgies, it is good to give full consideration to the consequences beforehand. You are taking on the responsibility for a living being for a lengthy period of time.

It is not my intention to talk you out of it, for you can get a lot of pleasure from one or more budgies. However, it is good to know what you are taking upon yourself. Keeping a pet means that you have to ensure that the animal has everything it needs. It cannot go off in search of food itself so it's dependent on you. For instance, do you have someone who can look after it while you are on vacation?

If you decide to continue with the purchase, there are several ways of doing this. The first might be to buy a bird in a pet store. Imported birds are no longer available, so all birds for sale have come from breeders. That is why most birds in the stores are banded. The second way is to buy a budgie at a bird show. Here you will find both dealers and fans who offer their birds for sale. The third and best method is to look for a good breeder and then, if possible, to visit his premises and choose one or more birds there. You will find the best breeders high up on the results lists at exhibitions which are held in the fall throughout the country. Nowadays the Internet also offers the possibility to search for breeders' sites. Several offer birds for sale and some of them have complete price lists.

The "English Budgie"
So-called English Budgies are often offered for sale in advertisements and in pet stores. What is meant by this term? The breeding and showing of budgies originated in England, and

between 1950 and 1970 very many budgies were exported to the European continent from England and thus became known as "English Budgies." These are valuable show birds, which breeders take to exhibitions.

If you do not intend to take part in exhibitions and competitions, you can get just as much pleasure out of keeping normal budgies. They are just as colorful; they are less powerful in build than the show birds; they often breed better than over-bred birds and they are usually much less expensive. All types of budgie are descended from the same wild forebear. Show birds are bigger and stronger solely because of constant selection for certain physical characteristics. Actually, the name "English Budgie" has become outdated.

Things to watch out for

No matter where you buy a bird, always make sure that you buy healthy birds which are as intact as possible. You cannot look inside a bird, but from the exterior you can often see that something is wrong with it. Pay attention to the following points in particular:

- A bird that looks at you with watery eyes and feathers sticking out is best not bought. It is not healthy.
- A healthy bird is lively, has its feathers close to its body, especially if you are standing directly in front of its cage, and the plumage is shiny.
- Furthermore, a bird for sale must be clean. It must not have dirty posterior feathers. That is an indication of bowel problems.
- The nose-point or "cere" must be smooth and shiny.
- A missing claw is not a disaster,

but birds with missing toes often cannot hold tight to their perch during mating, which leads to unfertilized eggs. So leave such birds in the store.

- A few missing feathers or broken quills need not be a problem, but the birds must be able to fly properly, so their wings must be complete.
- Pay attention to the cage the birds are kept in. Dirty, stuffy surroundings are a health risk.

Age
The age of the birds you plan to buy is important, particularly if you are buying birds for the first time and have little experience. It is best to buy young birds that have not yet been exposed to breeding. In pet stores in particular, you will find somewhat older birds for sale. You do not know the birds' backgrounds and they could be birds who cannot breed, or only with difficulty. Bear in mind that the good, longer-feathered birds can often only breed at the age of three to four. It is sometimes possible to buy good breeding pairs, but then you should buy them from a reputable source. If you are looking for birds you want to breed from immediately, choose birds that are about a year old. The age of banded birds can be found on the band, which contains, in addition to the breeding number, the name of the organization that issued the band, a serial number

and the year of issue.

If you want to buy a budgie to make it tame, choose as young a bird as possible. Young birds are independent at about 6 weeks and that is the best time to bring them home. This is the time when they can learn a lot, even to talk. When they are older, they learn with more difficulty and remain timid

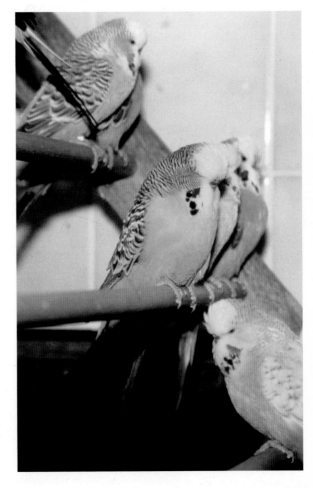

for longer. Young budgies with normal markings keep a striped forehead (which extends almost to the top of the beak) until the age of about 3 months. As they get older the stripes disappear and they get a clear (white or yellow) forehead and then only have the horizontal stripes on top of their head down as far as their necks. It is said that young males become most affectionate and learn to talk best.

Telling the difference between male and female

You can easily tell a bird's gender by its appearance. On males, the nose point above the beak (the cere), is blue and on females the nose point is brown. This applies to all so-called "fully coloreds" (completely pigmented birds). Mutations, for example, have differently colored ceres.

The cere does not fully color until the birds are 3 months old. Until that age all young birds, male and female, have almost the same brown cere. Yet there are differences. If you look closely, you will see that the young male's cere is a little bluish in color. In the young female it is brown, but directly next to the nostrils it is somewhat lighter, a whitish color. Another difference, which is not external, can be noticed if you take the birds in your hand. A female will bite more quickly and harder than a male.

parakeets budgerigar

Nutrition and feeding

In their natural habitat budgies live mainly off plant food, most of this being (grass) seeds which they peck from the ground. In the breeding season, they look for as many fresh or unripe seeds for their young as possible.

These contain plenty of vitamins and nutritional elements for the young birds and are digested easier than dry seeds. The female feeds recently hatched birds with crop milk. The male does not take part in this part of feeding the young, but feeds the female in the nest.

Feeding cage birds

Budgies as pets at home or on breeders' premises are fed by most owners with ready-to-eat seed mixtures from the stores. These seed mixtures contain different types of seeds, namely millet, canary seed, oats, linseed and a few sunflower seeds. The latter contain elements that tend to make birds fat, particularly in a small space in which they have too little exercise. For this reason, sunflower seeds should only be fed in moderation.

The complete mixtures are sold in pet stores in all kinds of packaging. The larger the packet the more economical it is. If you have only one bird, a two-pound packet will be enough for several weeks. Breeders with lots of birds buy their food in 50 pound sacks. Some breeders make their own mixture and buy the required seeds loose. This is not worth the effort for a single bird at home or for a few breeding pairs, and ready-to-eat mixtures from the stores are more than sufficient. Be sure to check the date on the package, and store food properly in a dark, dry place.

Additional food

Our budgies need more than just seeds to stay healthy. Additional food can be a diversion because the birds have something else to gnaw on.

Millet sprays

This is millet on the stalk and is the most important addition to the daily menu. It is somewhat fresher and softer than the millet in the seed mixture. Adult birds may have a piece no longer than 2 1/2 inches per day, otherwise they will get too fat. Providing millet sprays helps young budgies to feed themselves. Additionally the birds will have another nice diversion if you hang the millet from the top of the cage with a clothes pin. There are also special millet holders, which can be bought in pet stores.

Greens and fruit

You can try to find out what your birds enjoy most, but often you have to offer greens for several days before they realize that it is a tasty morsel. There are even tame budgies that did not realize that raw vegetables were tasty and healthy until their owner showed them how to eat them. Don't give up too quickly if your budgie takes a long time before it begins to eat raw vegetables. It is, and remains, a very important addition to the menu. Make sure the vegetables are well washed. Push large chunks of fruit through the bars of the cage. Soft fruit and leaf greens are best finely cut up and then put on a flat plate. Do not feed too much, just a small portion which they can eat in a fairly short time. Greens contain a lot of water and relatively few nutrients. It is important because it gives the birds something to do and because they sometimes want something other than seed. Too much can cause bowel problems such as diarrhea. Take whatever they have not eaten out of the cage again. It spoils quickly or starts to develop mildew.

Grass and weed seeds

Here too, you can try to find out what your birds particularly enjoy. Many different kinds of grass blades and weeds are suitable. In any case you can simply pick some blades of grass from your lawn. They will definitely like that and almost every backyard also has some so-called chickweed in it, a small green plant with very small white flowers. The stems contain a white milky fluid. You can also hang up a large bunch of grass and weed seeds, and watch how much your birds enjoy them and how it keeps them busy for hours. But be careful where you pick weeds and grass. In any event, do not pick them alongside a busy road because of the pollution from engine exhaust gases. Also, do not pick them from any land where pesticides have recently

Seeds

Millet

been used, either. Be sure to wash all greens in lukewarm water several times and let dry before feeding.

Sprouted seed

Sprouted seed is a good addition to the daily menu for young growing birds, birds that are molting, brooding birds and birds that do not want to eat greens and fruit.

How to prepare sprouted seed: Cover half a teaspoon of seed per bird (basic seed mixture, oatgerm or wheatgerm) with a three-quarter inch layer of water and let it soak for 24 hours.

Then rinse the seed well with lukewarm water, let it drip dry, put it in a glass dish and put a light covering over it. Let it stand for 48 hours in a light room at room temperature.

As soon as shoots start to emerge from the seeds, they can be fed to the bird. Rinse them in lukewarm water and let them drip dry first.

Food supplements

Apart from the above-mentioned foods, your birds need some food supplements.

Cuttlefish bone

Cuttlefish bone provides birds with calcium, which they need every day. A way of providing the birds with calcium is to give them cuttlebone (this is the backbone of a variety of squid). You can push this through the bars of the cage or hang it up inside the cage. Birds should always have access to extra calcium, especially during breeding season.

Grit

A mixture of oyster shells, limestone, mineral grit and sand provides essential grit to the birds. The grit remains in the gizzard and helps with the grinding down of seeds and digestion of food.

Iodine pellets

The only mineral necessary for health and not found naturally in a well-balanced diet is iodine. Iodine supplementation prevents thyroid problems and can be supplied through iodine pellets or through seeds soaked in iodine.

Vitamins and minerals

Whole books have been written about vitamins and minerals. They are vital for every living being. If there are deficiencies, diseases can develop, but overdoses can also cause problems. There is no harm in giving a dose of vitamins before the beginning of the breeding season, for example. Vitamins and minerals are also good for birds which are recovering from an illness or which have been eating poorly for a while. Give them a product which is specially designed for birds and which contains all the

necessary vitamins in the right proportions. In the normal course of events a bird that has been fed correctly will have received enough vitamins and minerals, and supplements should not be necessary. If you are not sure about the amount of vitamins and minerals in the feed you provide, you can always ask a veterinarian or an experienced breeder for advice, of course.

Water

Every living being consists mainly of water and clean daily drinking water is essential. A budgie drinks only a little water per day, but it is still necessary to clean its drinking bottle every day and to refill it with fresh water. It soon gets dirty and, especially in hot weather, mildew and bacteria can form which can make the bird ill. Algae can also form in the drinking bottle under the influence of light. The transparent part of the bottle slowly takes on a green or brown color. It looks dirty and it gives bacteria the chance to develop. Darker-colored drinking bottles, in which algae develop more slowly, are available in the stores. You can easily clean drinking bottles with a bottle-brush or by putting them in water with a chlorine solution for a few hours. Remember to rinse them thoroughly with clean water afterwards.

Daily care

In short, daily care consists of replenishing the drinking water

Cuttlefish bone

Water container

and feeding. Bear in mind that drinking bottles can leak. The seed trough has to be checked daily. The food trough sometimes appears to be full, but in reality it just contains empty seed husks. The birds peel the seed, leaving the empty husks behind. You can blow the empty husks out of the trough and then you can see how much seed is really left. When you go on vacation, remember to tell your "pet sitter" about this. It would not be the first time that things have gone wrong because the pet sitter was not properly instructed. I think that every pet store gets customers in the store during the summer period who are looking for a budgie that has to look just so, i.e., just like the poor animal that starved to death in the short period that they had to look after it. Also remove the uneaten greens, and sprouted seeds at least daily to prevent the growth of bacteria.

Part of daily care is also giving the necessary attention to your birds. You will find more about this in the chapter *Behavior and taming*

A home for your budgerigar

There are several different types of home for budgies. People who want to have budgies as pets usually keep their birds in a cage in the living room.

Devotees who are good with their hands can construct their own indoor aviary, and the real fanatic has an extensive outdoor aviary.

In the living room

Budgies can be kept without any noteworthy problems in the living room. Cages can be bought in all shapes and sizes in the stores. However, with a little Do-It-Yourself skill you can build a suitable cage yourself. Bear in mind the following in connection with budgies in the home:
If you don't want to run the risk of feathers, sand or empty seed husks landing on the floor, it's best to keep the cage outside, with proper shelter and if weather permits. Birds make a bit of a mess, but that is almost unavoidable and you can gather it up from directly underneath or in front of the cage, so that it won't get spread all over your living room.

Budgies exude substances from their feathers to which some people can be allergic. People who suffer from allergies to feathers or feather dust should not keep parakeets.

The number of birds you want to keep in it defines the size of the cage or indoor aviary. Whatever the number, make sure that your birds have enough room to fly. A budgie is by nature not such a climber as an Agapornis (lovebird) or a Catharine Parakeet. That's why they need room to fly. A tall narrow cage is therefore less suitable than a cage with more length. Birds usually fly horizontally and not steeply upwards. Do not fill a cage with all kinds of toys that restrict flying space either. A suitable cage should be at least 20 inches long for one budgie and at least 27 inches long for two.

A place for the cage

Place the cage in a well-lit place in your living room, but not in front of the window where your bird will be in full sunlight all day. Birds like sunlight but they have to be able to decide for themselves when they want to sit in the shade, and it can quickly get very hot behind a window. The best place is against a wall, for example. Here they feel safer because the other inhabitants of the house can only approach the cage from one side. If birds are in a place which people can walk around from different directions, they cannot withdraw and thus they feel less secure. Make sure your birds are not in a draft, as this does not suit them at all. Also make sure that the cage stands firmly on a table, a stand or a wall fixture. A cage that hangs on a chain, swaying with every movement of the budgie, gives the bird an uneasy feeling and will make it more timid.

Equipping the cage

Make sure there are enough perches, which are firmly attached. Too many perches limit the flying space needed. Perches must be thick enough for the budgie to grasp around them. The best idea is to install perches of differing widths. That is better for their leg muscles. Sometimes the perches supplied with a cage are thin pieces of plastic. For very little money you can replace them with wooden perches from a pet store with, for example, a diameter of 0.4 to 0.5 inches. You can also use willow twigs. But remember that your budgies will gnaw on them, so that they will have to be replaced after a while. But your budgies are kept occupied and that is very important. Furthermore, the fresh wood contains substances that are good for a budgie's health.

It is also important to hang a number of toys in the cage, such as a mirror or a swing with bells. Of course you can use your own imagination and make toys yourself. But bear the safety of your birds in mind. Make sure that they have enough room to fly and that they cannot get caught up in or crash into the toys. These toys are especially important if you are often away from home or only have a single budgie.

It is best to use standard cage sand on the floor of a cage kept in the living room. This usually contains grit, which the birds like to pick up. There are so many different types of floor litter these days and each has its own

At the breeder

wings one by one. Once your budgie has become completely used to bathing, you can put a flat bathing dish on the floor of the cage/aviary. Your bird will then really enjoy a long bath.

Make sure that your bird can easily find the food and water containers or bottles. Especially when a bird comes into a new cage, it sometimes has difficulty in finding its food. Put some loose food on the floor of the cage. That will help it to get used to its new situation.

The outdoor aviary

If you are so fortunate as to have enough room outside to build an aviary in your backyard, you should be aware of several limiting factors. The policy of local authorities varies from place to place. Get the necessary information before you start building. It could also be important to discuss the matter with your neighbors.

A suitable aviary consists of an exterior run with permanent night quarters. As budgies are colony birds, you can also build an aviary and keep several pairs of budgies there with or without other birds. Suitable birds to keep with budgies are Cockatiels, Bourkes Parakeets and the more robust members of the finch family, which can look after themselves well, such as Paddy Birds and Zebra Finches.

advantages and disadvantages. Ask the storekeeper for advice. Sometimes people advise the use of newspaper as floor covering because it absorbs a lot of moisture and is easy to replace. The disadvantage is the printing ink used, which is harmful to both people and animals.

Budgies also like to take a bath. For this purpose, you can hang a cage birdbath in front of the opening to the cage or aviary with a half-inch of lukewarm water in it. It will take a while before your bird has conquered its fear of the new object, before it goes in for extensive bathing. The bird will first sit on the edge and carefully drink some water and get its beak and breast wet. If it enjoys this, it will carefully sit in the water up to its belly and then submerge its

A place for the aviary

The size and place for your aviary is determined of course by the space at hand. If you can choose, an aviary that faces east or west is the best place. Facing south it is in the full sunshine and facing north it will soon be too dark and cold in the winter.

Prevent overexposure to strong sunlight but also to wind and rain at the cold time of year. Most outdoor aviaries for budgies have a roof, which can be transparent. This keeps the aviary dry and prevents the floor or perches becoming fouled by the excrement of wild birds. It also gives more protection against birds of prey and cats, etc.

Building materials

You can use different materials to build an aviary. These days, aviaries are often made from rectangular aluminum pipes. Stores have all kinds of joints for sale so that building is easy for a Do-It-Yourselfer. The material is fairly expensive but needs little maintenance. Wood is a cheaper material. It is very suitable, but it needs more maintenance and has to be protected against the budgies' urge to gnaw. This can be solved by fixing mesh to the interior so that it is more difficult for the birds to reach the wood.

You can buy the mesh by the yard or by the roll in the larger specialty bird stores or in the ironmongery department of your DIY store. Mesh for budgies does not have to be very heavy grade. The mesh is usually galvanized to prevent rust. New mesh is very shiny, which can be a bit of a problem. You can treat it with dark paint that is harmless to birds. This gives you a better view of the birds but also ensures that the mesh lasts longer. Choose mesh with gaps that are small enough to prevent the budgies crawling through (gaps of less

than 1/2"). I also recommend that the mesh should be such that sparrows and other wild birds cannot get through, spreading disease and eating the food.

The floor of an outdoor aviary for budgies must be very dry. A wet floor is a medium for bacteria. Plants are not really necessary in an aviary for budgies because of their urge to gnaw, but they do make it look really attractive and they offer the birds a natural distraction. The floor need not be completely earthen. The part where there are no plants can consist of dry sand, gravel or even just concrete – as long as the drainage is good.

Equipping the outdoor aviary
When equipping an outdoor aviary for budgies it is best to reckon on including the same items as in a cage. You can make perches yourself from dowel rods, which can be bought in various lengths at hardware stores. Many fans make wall-bars from them with several perches placed at an angle under each other (see photos). There must be enough places for the birds to sit in an aviary, but room to fly is just as important. An intriguingly-formed branch or log in the aviary is decorative and gives your birds something to do, because they can gnaw at it.

Bear in mind that birds like to sleep as high as possible. If there is too little room, they may fight. Because of the danger of nocturnal disturbance in the aviary caused by birds of prey and cats, it is best to get your birds used to spending the night in their night quarters. The night quarters should therefore be higher than the outdoor run and have high perches and a window so that it remains light as long as possible in the evening. They will then automatically look inside for a safe place to sleep. If that does

not work, you may want to lock your birds up in the night quarters before dark. Remember that it is the (seating) space in the night quarters which determines the number of birds you can keep in the aviary itself.

The night quarters must give access via one or more doors to the aviary. Make sure that these doors can be opened from outside the aviary. That way you do not have to enter the aviary to open or close them. Cover the windows with mesh so that the birds cannot fly into them at top speed. The mesh also prevents the birds escaping should a windowpane get broken for any reason. You can put a door between the night quarters and the outdoor aviary. An exterior door as part of an outdoor aviary presents the risk of birds escaping, unless you build a porch around it.

It is best to situate the feeding, drinking and bathing areas indoors. You can put them on the ground but it is better if they are placed higher. That way they are less liable to be fouled by the birds and any vermin such as mice won't be able to reach them as easily. When you release birds into your aviary, put them into the night quarters, where they can find their food immediately, and not straight into the outdoor aviary. Release your birds as early in the day as possible and not just before nightfall. That way they have enough time to get to know their new quarters and to find their food and drink.

Heating

It is not strictly necessary to heat an outdoor aviary for your birds to spend the winter there. As long as they have dry, protected night quarters, they can easily do without heating. Cold is less of a problem for them than the cold dampness we so often have in winter. If you do use heating, make sure it does not get too dry in your aviary. Especially in brooding time, a humidity of 60-65% is necessary for the eggs to hatch normally. If it is too dry, the film around the embryo hardens and the chicks cannot free themselves from the egg.

Lighting

Sufficient light is important. Your birds will slowly pine away in a place that is too dark and you will not have good breeding results. In most cases you will need to supplement the daylight with artificial light in the form of lighting tubes. With the aid of timers, you can ensure that the light goes on and off at the same time every day. This ensures a natural regularity in the length of daylight. If you have to switch the lights on and off manually, the birds' length of daylight will fluctuate, which in turn

upsets their body clock. They may suddenly start molting or abandon their nests. It is best to have the lights going on and off at the same time every day. The recommended length of a bird's day is 13 to 15 hours. It is advisable to use automatic dimmers, so that the change from light to darkness is not too sudden. Dimmers ensure that the light goes on and off gradually.

The breeding cage

If you have decided to breed your birds, it is advisable to have breeding cages, in which you can keep pairs of birds. Of course you can leave it up to the birds themselves in the aviary colony, but it can happen that the birds which are not brooding disturb those that are, causing them to leave the nest or peck open other birds' eggs.

Breeding cages can easily be made by a good Do-It-Yourselfer. You can get materials for them in all kinds of sizes. I prefer white, plasticized chipboard, which is good for building with and which is later easy to keep clean. Untreated chipboard harbors gasses, which are given off for a long time by the glue used in its production. This is bad for your birds. You can also use plywood, which is good for building with, but which has to be painted with bird-friendly paint. It is more

difficult to keep clean and you will have to repaint it now and then. The advantage is that you can use a color other than white, which has a more calming effect on the birds.

The most popular breeding cages are closed on all sides except one, the front. You can make the front panel yourself out of metal or mesh. But most budgie fans use ready-made front panels, which can be bought in varying sizes and models. They are equipped with little doors and sometimes also flaps for plastic feeding troughs. These are not so suitable for budgies. The birds are a bit too big for them. A porcelain or earthenware feeding trough on the floor of the cage is a much better solution. However, these front panels are very suitable for hanging drinking bottles from.

The minimum measurements for a breeding cage are 20"x16"x16" (length x width x height), but the bigger the better is the rule, especially when the young arrive. Attaching the nesting log to the outside of the cage leaves the maximum space in the cage for the birds themselves.

If you intend to build cages yourself, I advise you to buy the front panels first and only to begin building the cages when you have the exact measurements. Try to make the cages in such a way that the budgies cannot gnaw at the wood too easily. The rough sides of the material used can be covered with aluminum or plastic strips, which can be bought to fit most thicknesses of chipboard.

If you are not a handyman, you can choose from a wide range of

prefabricated cages. These are not cheap, but they are an investment that will give you pleasure for years to come. They can be assembled by anyone, without even picking up a hammer or screwdriver, and can be equally easily taken apart again should the need arise. These system cages are often fitted with removable partitions. By removing them, you can increase the space available for the birds. The most popular floor covering in brooding cages is aviary sand. It is advisable to place a sand tray in the cage, which can easily be removed for cleaning. A metal tray is the most convenient. If you make the cages yourself, you should bear in mind that sand and seed remains may get stuck between the sand tray and the walls. If you make the tray an exact fit, you will find it very difficult to get it out again to clean it.

Holding cages

You can make any number and size of these, all depending on how much space you have. They are used for separating those young birds that have become independent and allowing them to grow up in surroundings that are more spacious than the breeding cages. They are also used for letting brooding birds regain their fitness before the following breeding season or before they return to the colony. So if you want to keep males and females separate in the rest period, you should make at least two holding cages. As far as the equipment is concerned, please see the section covering the night quarters of the aviary.

Holding cages

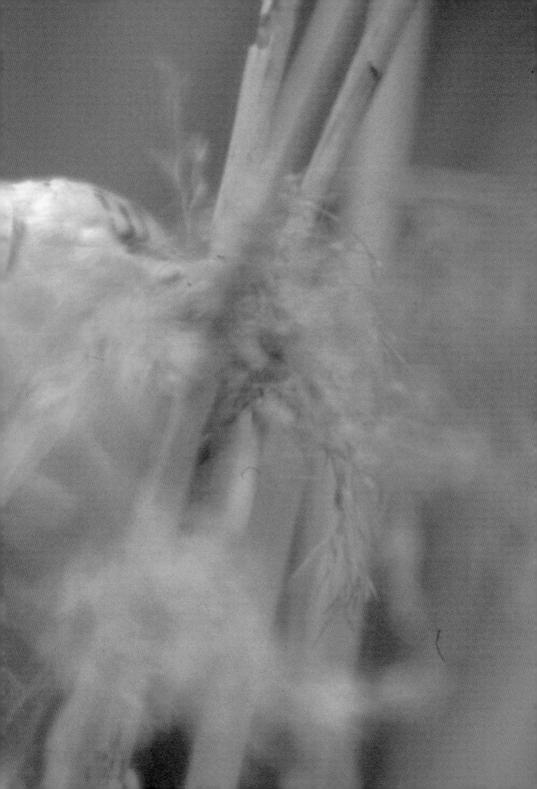

Behavior and taming

The budgie is one of the most popular pet birds. The reasons for this are obvious. These birds are relatively easy to look after, they are lively and available in many different colors.

Aviary birds

One of their most endearing qualities is that they are docile and affectionate. With a little patience and luck, they can even learn to talk.

Behavior in the wild
A budgie is by nature a very social creature. In Australia, they live and brood in colonies. They are the most tranquil members of the parrot family in Australia. They spend the hottest part of the day in the high tops of eucalyptus trees. As they are not noisy and have a good camouflage color (their natural color is light green), the colonies often go unnoticed when they are sitting high up in the trees.

Budgies forage early in the morning and towards the evening, because it's cooler at those times. During the day they rest as much as possible in order to conserve body water. An animal (humans, too) needs less moisture when it is resting. The budgies feed on different kinds of grass seeds and some green plants (grasses). At night, the temperature can drop below freezing, and drops of dew can be found on the leaves of plants in the morning. In periods of drought budgies use these drops as drinking water. If drinking water is readily available, budgies will drink every three hours.

It sometimes does not rain for months in Central Australia. In the end, the grasses and plants wither completely and watering places dry up. To a colony of budgies this is the signal to move on to another area where food and water can be found. This can mean that a colony sometimes has to fly hundreds of miles. These treks are often undertaken by large flocks of budgies, just like those undertaken by starlings in our latitudes. During the trek, the budgies communicate with each other by using certain calls.

Budgies in captivity

As we saw, budgies in their natural habitat live in groups. If you want to keep budgies as pets, you should take this into account. They are used to company and do not like being alone. If they cannot find one of their own kind, they will associate with another bird or with humans. If you decide to keep a single budgie as a pet, you will have to give your bird enough attention. You will be replacing, as it were, its own kind. This means that you really have to busy yourself in and around the house all day so that your bird can keep you in its sights and can

have contact with you from a distance. If you cannot give enough time and attention to your budgie, it is better to buy two. Although they will take somewhat more time to become tame and become attached to you, they will have each other's company.

In aviaries, budgies can be kept in colonies or together with other birds. At breeding time they will fight over the best nesting place, but once that is sorted out things are usually okay. Of the parrot species, Cockatiels and Bourkes Parakeets are well suited for keeping together with budgies. As far as other types of birds are concerned, you could consider Paddy Birds, Zebra Finches, Diamond Finches, etc.

Whatever you do, avoid overpopulating an aviary and make sure there are enough perches and nesting boxes (preferably double the number of pairs of birds in the aviary). Ensure that there are several

very probably looks completely different from the trough in the cage they were born in. Spread some food in the cage before you put the bird in and include some millet too. Then they will soon find something to eat. Leave the newcomer alone for a while so that it can soon feel at ease. It is advisable not to put a new bird in a new cage too late in the day. The earlier it is, the more time the bird has to get used to it surroundings.

Quietly try to get the bird used to you. You will see that if you speak in a quiet voice to your bird, it will soon react and start listening. If their owners behave calmly, birds will quickly get used to them and will be calm themselves. After a little while, your budgie will no longer try to creep away and may already approach you.

feeding places. Some dominant birds may occupy the feeding trough and drive all the birds away, which come near it. The weaker birds can't feed and will starve.

Settling in

With the right care and treatment you will get a lot of pleasure from owning a tame budgie. Try to get as young a bird as possible. At the age of 6 to 7 weeks, young budgies are just independent enough to feed themselves, and that is a good time to put them in a cage without their parents. Give them enough time to get used to the cage and its surroundings. During this period you should be quiet when near the cage. Your birds may not find the food trough immediately, because it

Taming

Owing to their social nature, budgies are particularly suited to taming and can possibly be taught tricks too. However, they must be completely accustomed to you first. After a time you can try and see if your budgie will sit on your hand. You can do this by giving the budgie its daily millet in your hand rather than just pushing it through the bars of the cage. If you lure it in this way, the temptation will be greater than its fear of your hand. If the bird sits on

your hand in order to reach the millet, the battle is already half won, and at a later stage it will also sit on your finger. Talk very softly to your bird while doing this.

One budgie is not the same as another, and that means that the one takes longer to become tame than the other. Never ever lose your patience, because then you have to start all over again. If you try to catch your bird to put it on your hand, you will fail. Being caught will make the bird timid. In any case always offer the bird the back of your hand, as most budgies find the palm of the hand frightening. You will finally be able to get the bird in and out of its cage by letting it sit on your hand.

Flying free

Once your budgie has completely got used to its cage and trusts you completely, it's time to let it have a good fly around the room. But beforehand you will have to take several measures to prevent mishaps:
• Shut all windows and doors so that your budgie cannot escape.
• It is better to draw the drapes closed during the first flights.
• Only when the bird has got used to flying in the room can you gradually increase the size of uncovered areas of glass. In so doing, you will reduce the risk

of the bird flying into them.
- Make sure that your bird does not eat poisonous plants.
- Make sure that it does not gnaw at electric cables.
- Make sure that your bird can't get caught up in certain places in the room, such as between two cupboards, in the wastepaper basket, behind the bookcase, in buckets or in a sink with water and suds, on sources of heat and flames, such as candles and open fires.
- Do not get the bird out of its cage before its first flight in order to force it to fly, but give it the time to launch into its first flight from the cage. It will probably climb up onto the top of its cage first to have a good look around.

Flying is not usually a problem once the bird has conquered its initial fears. The next step that your budgie has to learn is landing. The following situations can occur here:
- Your budgie lands back on top of its cage. Let the bird decide itself if it wants to fly again. When your bird has had enough, it will climb back into its cage itself, especially if there's something tasty inside.
- Your budgie lands on the ground. In their natural habitat budgies forage on the ground and they feel quite at ease doing this. Put some seeds on the ground and then put the cage close to the budgie. If food is on

Houseplants that are poisonous for budgies
Primula (*primrose)*
Mistletoe
Wax plant
Amaryllis
Azalea
Boxwood
Poinsettia
Crown of thorns (*Euphorbia milii)*
Dieffenbachia (all varieties)
Yew (*Taxus)*
Hyacinth
Periwinkle (*Vinca minor)*
Nightshade (*the whole nightshade family, including petunia)*
Narcissus
Oleander
Ardisia berries
Christmas rose
Laurel (*Codiaeum variegatum)*
Ornamental asparagus

the ground, the budgie will soon want to go back into its familiar cage, especially if more food is to be found there.
- Your budgie lands on a high cupboard, in the drapes or a lamp. Returning to the cage is now a little more complicated, for a budgie feels safest up high and will not be that keen on leaving the place very quickly. Try to lure the bird with some millet and by talking to it. If this does not work, and the budgie has already been at its lookout post for half an hour without showing any intention

of going back to its cage, you can hold the cage right in front of it, so that it can climb back in. If this also fails, leave it where it is and leave it alone. Make sure it can easily reach its cage and that it can find something tasty there. Sooner or later the bird will return to its cage. In the meantime keep a close eye on all doors and windows.

What you should **NOT** do:

• Never let your budgie fly for the first time when you have only a little time yourself. Realize it

parakeets budgerigar

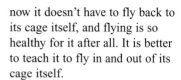

now it doesn't have to fly back to its cage itself, and flying is so healthy for it after all. It is better to teach it to fly in and out of its cage itself.

Boredom

For budgies, just as for the larger parrot varieties, boredom is unhealthy. Life in a cage is not exactly challenging for a pair of budgies. They do not have to make an effort to find food, they do not have to flee from predators, they do not have to fight to find a partner and they do not often have to invest time and energy in brooding.

Lonely budgies try to find consolation in (to human eyes) totally insignificant objects. It sometimes happens that in the case of a long period of boredom a budgie suffers such mental distress that it starts plucking its own feathers. Scientists are not completely certain why they do this, but it is obviously harmful to the bird. If your budgie starts plucking at its feathers, get help from a veterinarian.

may take a while before your budgie returns to its cage.
• Never chase your bird trying to catch it or catch it by throwing a cloth over it. This would seriously damage your bird's trust in you and the surroundings and, next time, this will not work at all.

Once your bird has learned to sit on your finger, you can of course "pick it up" from its lookout post by letting it step from there onto your finger. Then you can take it back to its cage. However, you spoil the bird by doing this, as

Toys

To avoid boredom, make sure that your budgies have budgie toys available. This is especially important if you have a single budgie, but it is also vital for a pair of budgies. Budgies are intelligent birds, which are presented with constant challenges in their natural habitat. That is why they also need challenges in captivity. The best-loved toys are:

- Bells, above all because they shine.
- Mirrors are irresistible to budgies. Time and again a budgie will try to push away its imagined rival and then jump to one side so that the rival (the mirror) cannot push it off the perch.
- A plastic dummy bird. Females try to feed it and males try to get rid of the rival or regard it as a surrogate female and try courting it.
- Little balls in the cage or outside. Budgies like playing with these, especially if you take part, too.
- Budgies like swinging in the cage. There are lots of different swings or climbing ropes to be had in pet stores.
- Budgies like gnawing, especially the females when they are not brooding. Regularly give your birds twigs from non-poisonous plants to gnaw on. Pieces of cuttlebone and other gnawing material (pet store) will always be appreciated.

Always make sure that budgies cannot get caught up in toys hanging in the cage!

Personal attention
Tame budgies like being close to their familiar caregiver. Make time for your budgie every day and let it sit on your hand. Talk to it and encourage it to imitate words and tunes. You can also try to stroke the bird in places it cannot reach itself. Allow it to get used to your finger by beginning with a spot on the wings. The bird will probably fairly quickly let you stroke its neck or its head. When the bird has become completely accustomed to this, it will probably want to groom you too. With great tenderness it will clean your eyelashes, eyebrows and skin by nibbling at them gently.

Teaching budgies to talk
Many budgies learn to say a few

words. Often they repeat words they frequently hear such as greetings, names, curses and "hello." Some can say whole sentences. In order to teach something systematically to a budgie, you can try the following. Do this when you are alone with the bird so that it is less easily distracted:

• Say the appropriate words in situations that occur frequently. For example. "Good morning" when you come into a room in the morning or "Good night" when you put the light out at night or "nice" when you give it something to eat.
• Always say the words or the short sentence in the same tone and with the same rhythm and whenever your budgie looks at you full of expectation.
• Every day, sing or whistle short melodies in front of your budgie, but not too many different ones.

• Once your budgie already knows a few words and melodies, repeat its repertoire every day so that it can remember everything and perfect the pronunciation.
• Record the repertoire on a tape. You can then play it when the bird has to be on its own or just to practice.

Some talented talkers can say fitting sentences in certain situations. This often happens by chance, and we discover that our birds have learned much more than we imagined. So you could be in for a few surprises!

It is said that male budgies learn to talk better than females and that they are also faster to tame. They can also copy a woman's voice better than a man's. Success is dependent on the time you can devote to your budgie and the way you treat your bird.

Breeding

In the wild, the beginning of the brooding season depends on the availability of enough food and water, and begins as soon as the days start to get longer. In Australia, that is at the end of the rainy season or shortly thereafter.

In the regions where budgies breed most, it rains irregularly and usually only in the rainy season.

When it rains again after a period of drought, nature quickly comes back to life again. Plants begin to grow again and the grass becomes greener and produces seeds. The insect world also comes completely back to life.
During such a period, there is food in abundance for birds, and budgies benefit from this too.

Breeding in the wild
Budgies normally live in large groups but in the breeding season they form couples, which go off in search of a suitable nesting hole in a tree. Once they have found a suitable nest, they spend most of their time there. The female gnaws here and there to get the nest just right. The nest is not covered with nest material; at most there is some finely gnawed wood left in the nest as a floor covering.

When mating has taken place, the female lays the first egg after about 10 days. The subsequent eggs are laid every other day. The total number of eggs varies from about four to eight eggs. Normally a single mating is sufficient to fertilize all the eggs. The sperm cells stay alive in the female's body long enough to fertilize all the ripening egg cells. The female usually starts brooding after laying the second egg. After 19-21 days, usually early in the morning, the first chick hatches or the first two if the female did not start brooding until the second egg. The other

chicks hatch every other day.

The female feeds the chicks for the first few days with so-called crop milk, a highly protein-rich secretion of the gizzard wall. The males do not produce crop milk so they are not involved in feeding chicks in the early days. If the young all were to hatch on the same day, the female would not be able to produce enough crop milk to be able to feed them all. So nature has taken perfect care of everything. After about a week, the male starts to help with the feeding. In the natural habitat this will be unripe fresh (grass) seeds. Young budgies fly out of the nest in about their fourth week of life, coming back in the evening to spend the night there. After about 5 to 6 weeks, the young are independent and are no longer completely dependent on their parents. They beg for food now and then, but gradually they look after themselves more and more.

The breeding season in the aviary

For birds in an outdoor aviary the breeding period begins at the end of March or beginning of April, depending on the weather. You are in control of everything as far as light and heating are concerned and that is why it is more the breeder's decision when the breeding season begins. However, it is not the case that you decide when the breeding season begins

and your birds are automatically ready for it at that moment. You have to prepare your birds for the breeding season by making sure that the length of daylight is the same as the length of daylight at the beginning of the natural breeding season. Your birds must also not be lacking in nutrients. A breeding bird needs to be healthy and fit at the start of the breeding season. It must have had enough time to regain its strength after the previous breeding season and /or be fully-grown. Give your birds plenty of food, possibly enriched with cod liver oil, on a daily basis before the breeding season and give them a dose of vitamins if necessary. Ensure that they have enough calcium, etc.

If you have to make any modifications to the cages or aviary, do this before the beginning of the breeding season, for once the birds are sitting on their eggs, they are easily disturbed by noise. Put your breeding cage in order as well before you begin. An extra cleaning session will do no harm. Check for any vermin such as blood lice or mice and take any necessary steps.

Putting a pair together

If you want to breed special colors from your budgies, choosing the pairs for breeding is an important task. If you just want a nest of birds for the fun of it, it does not

matter which birds mate with each other. But you must remember of course to put a male and female together in a brooding cage, otherwise not an awful lot is going to happen. (See the chapter: *Buying a budgie;* Telling the difference between males and females.) Perhaps your birds have got there before you and have already chosen a mate themselves. It is advisable to take a few things into account so that the breeding can take place as smoothly as possible.

Age

Do not use birds that are younger than one year. Also birds that have grown too old, older than 5 years, can have problems with breeding.

Health

Only use healthy birds for breeding. Their ceres and eyes shine. They are lively. They must not be fat. You can sometimes tell if a bird is overweight by ruffling the breast and belly feathers while the bird is in your hand.

Courtship and mating

If you have a pair of budgies, you can tell by their behavior whether they get along with each other. The male constantly tries to approach the female, which, in its turn, accepts this and perhaps reacts positively. If the birds pet each other and the male feeds the female, then they are quite definitely getting along well with each other. But that does not necessarily mean that they will actually get as far as breeding. Sometimes the birds become just good friends, but not partners. In the wild, the choice of partner is very important to budgies. Our budgies at home do not have so much choice. If your pair is not interested in breeding, you can put a second male in the cage. That often makes the female broody, because she can now choose between two males. What you must never do is put a second female in the cage because in the wild, it is the females that compete with each other for the males. They would start fighting, which could lead to very bloody situations.

As soon as the female reacts positively to the male's advances, the male will start trying to impress her in many different ways. He may fly about wildly, play too vigorously with the toys, make his neck and head feathers stand up, strut back and forth and lovingly play "cheek-to-cheek" with the female. During all this the male will constantly chatter away in budgie language. For quite a while, the female seems unmoved by all this, but then she suddenly offers herself by sticking her tail up in the air and tipping her head back. Very cautiously, kissing her all the time, the male climbs onto the female's back. He holds tight to the female's neck feathers and puts one wing around her. Then the male rubs his cloaca for a short time against the female's, which causes his sperm to enter her oviduct.

Brooding

When you have put two budgies together that seem to be a pair, give them a nesting log or a nesting box. Even if the birds have not yet mated, they can still get used to the nesting log. If you put the nesting log in the aviary among the other birds, you must ensure that the other birds do not use it, preventing the female from being able to lay her eggs anywhere. That is why breeding cages are usually used, ensuring that the pair can brood undisturbed. The nesting log is a large block of wood, a birch trunk, for example, most of which is hollowed out, so that the eggs can lie in it. You can put some nest material in, but usually the female will do this herself. But do make sure that you provide nest material in the brooding cage or the aviary. There is a lid on the nesting log, which makes it easier to check the nest. If you check the nest regularly from the beginning, your birds will quickly get used to this and will not feel disturbed later when they are brooding. When you check the nest, you can note the date the first egg is laid. Then you will know when to expect it to hatch. You can also note the number of eggs and whether they are fertilized, etc. You can tell a

fertilized egg by its color. It becomes milky-white, whereas the light shines pinkish through an unfertilized egg. As the embryo starts to develop in the egg, you can see the heart and the blood vessels by holding it against the light.

The eggs are laid about 8 days after mating and the female starts brooding immediately. She will lay one egg every other day up to a maximum of five eggs.

Growth of the young

If all goes well, the eggs hatch after 19-21 days. The chicks are first fed by the female with crop milk, later the male will also help with feeding. The male makes sure that the female gets enough to eat. Ensure that your birds get used to the cod liver oil-enriched feed long before this time, and do not start providing this only when the chicks have hatched. After about 4 weeks the young fly out for the first time, but they go back to the block regularly and like spending the night there.

When they are about 6 weeks old, the young birds can feed themselves and can be regarded as independent. At this time they can be taken away from their parents so that the latter can start a new brood. However, do not take the young away until you have seen them eating and thus can be sure that they are independent. Not all budgies are independent at the same age. When you take the young away from their parents, it is best to put them together in a holding cage so that they can become completely independent there. After that, simply put them with the other birds in the aviary.

If the young birds were born in the aviary itself, they can stay there.

After the young have been taken away, the parent birds usually start breeding again. Make sure that the pair do not breed all year round but limit the number of sessions to two, three at the most. Give the birds a few months rest afterwards so that they don't get exhausted. Then you will have a lot of pleasure out of your birds for another year.

Breeding problems

The breeding process does not always run as smoothly as

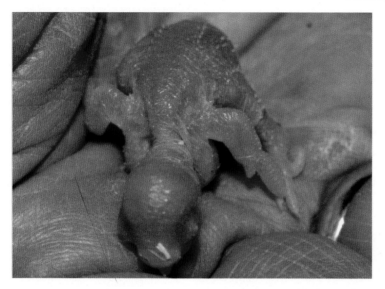

Few days old

described here. Problems can sometimes occur. Always try to find out what is wrong by observing your birds carefully. If unfertilized eggs have been laid, possible causes are:

- The pair chosen by you does not hit it off. Split the pair up if they cannot get used to each other.
- The birds are too young. Put them back in the aviary for a while and try again later, or split the couple up and put them with older partners.
- The mating failed due to loose perches.
- The posterior feathers are too long, which can prevent fertilization. Cut some of the plumage away.
- The eggs are fertilized but do not hatch because the cage is too dry, but sometimes also because of too high humidity. The recommended humidity is 55%-65%.
- Eggs are opened and leak because the parents' nails are too long.
- Eggs are laid but the female does not want to brood. You can transfer the eggs to a pair that broods well.
- The young are not fed or fed badly. In this case, too, transferring them to a nest with young of about the same age can be the solution. Transferring is also advisable if a nest only contains one or two young. A nest of three or more young often thrives better. The chicks keep each other warm.
- The young are attacked, usually by the father. Put a protective roof in the brooding cage that the chicks can creep under.

Competitions

In many countries, budgie competitions are very popular. The sport entails breeders trying to breed all different kinds of colors from their expensive English budgies.

Most breeders have set up special breeding lines for this. The different colors are achieved by diverse mutations of the genetic factors of the original budgies. Wonderful colors have been produced by many years of selection.

When a breeder has achieved the desired breeding result he can have his bird(s) judged at an exhibition where breeders can win prizes. The color patterns have to conform to a certain standard for budgies. It would go beyond the aims of this book to go into more detail about this. For more information you can get in touch with one of the organizations listed at the back of this book.

Your budgerigar's health

Fortunately, budgies are not particularly susceptible to diseases. But overbred exhibition birds are often weaker and thus more susceptible to all kinds of ailments.

Some frequently occurring diseases and ailments that can affect budgies are dealt with in this chapter.

Signs of a sick bird
A sick bird can best be recognized by its behavior:
• It is less lively.
• It sleeps a lot.
• Its feathers stick out. It sits in a ball shape.
• The eyes are dull and watery.
• It has often lost weight because it eats little or nothing and the breastbone can clearly be felt through the skin.
• It avoids contact.
• It drinks more than normal.
• Its excrement is thinner than normal and may smell bad, too.

If you suspect that one of your birds is sick, it's best to put it in a separate cage in warm and quiet surroundings. Consult a veterinarian as soon as possible. Delayed treatment can result in fatal consequences. Cover your budgie's cage well on the way to the veterinarian's so that it doesn't become chilled. The veterinarian will perform a physical examination and/or laboratory tests and suggest appropriate treatments.

Prevention
Treating birds is not a simple matter, so prevention is better. Here is a list of points, which can represent a risk for your bird.

General preventative measures
• Make sure that cats and dogs cannot get into your budgie's

cage. If you let your budgie out of the cage, make sure that the cat or dog is not in the same room.

- Be careful not to step on a budgie that has been let out of its cage.
- Prevent excessive growth of nails and beak by using perches of differing thickness and by providing sufficient things to gnaw on (twigs, iodine block). Give your budgie only its own food and do not feed it on your leftovers. Fats and sugars are harmful to its health.
- Do not let your bird become chilled, make sure it is not in a draft.
- Prevent parasitic infections (lice, mites, and worms) by keeping cages and equipment very clean. Seek veterinary care immediately if a parasite is suspected.
- In general you can prevent many diseases by paying strict attention to hygiene. Make sure the cages and feeding and drinking troughs are clean. You can avoid a lot of distress this way. If a bird's wings or legs are broken, it is best to consult a veterinarian immediately.

Nails

If your bird's nails have to be clipped, use good nail scissors. Hold the claw to the light so that you can see where the blood vessel is. Make sure you do not damage this. If the trimmed nail does start to bleed, try to stop the bleeding by applying corn starch or styptic powder to the end of it.

Molting

Every year, birds exchange their suit of feathers for a new one. The old, worn feathers fall out and new ones grow. This process normally takes place at the end of the summer and lasts about 6 weeks. It is a natural process that is part of every bird's life. It sometimes causes them to be a little less active, but they are soon back to normal. If you make sure they regularly get enough sprouted seeds and supplemented feed at this time, the molt will take its orderly course and you will soon have a handsome bird again. Young birds molt within a few weeks of becoming independent. They

exchange their young plumage for their adult suit of feathers and then display their full coloring. The matte colors are replaced by the attractive bright colors of the adult bird.

Scaly face (or scaly leg)

Sometimes budgies develop a crusty, scaly cere. This can be an

infection known as "scaly face." It is caused by a parasite, a mite that tunnels itself into the host. Severe cases cause severe beak deformities and can spread to the legs. It can be combated with a fatty substance that is smeared onto the cere. Various ointments for this purpose can be bought at the pet store. The effect of the ointment is that the mite's tunnels are sealed, which causes the mite to die. A veterinarian can also treat this disease with an injectable medication. Do not wait too long with treatment, as the infection can easily be passed on to other budgies. Budgies regularly rub their beaks along the perches and in this way other birds are infected. If your birds are infected, treat them immediately but also clean their perches thoroughly with a diluted bleach solution.

Psittacosis (also called parrot disease, ornithosis, or chiamydiosis)

Psittacosis is a disease caused by an organism called chlamydia psittaci. It is rare in parakeets, but it is important because it can be transmitted to humans. Infected birds show signs of respiratory disease along with runny eyes and slimy, green droppings. The signs are fairly non-specific, and diagnosis is difficult. Your veterinarian will discuss appropriate treatment options, including prevention of the spread of psittacosis to other birds and to humans.

French Molt

French Molt is a disease that can only occur in budgies, causing the plumage to be incompletely formed, which means that the bird cannot fly. The disease can be diagnosed as early as in young birds that are still in the nest. Budgies suffering from French Molt must be kept apart from other budgies, because the disease is very contagious. It is especially important to protect brooding pairs from this disease, as otherwise the young can catch it. Medications do not help in this case as they do not help to restore the plumage. A bird with French Molt will never be able to fly, which is why these birds are called crawlers. But they can become very tame, often because they have to be housed alone.

Treating sick birds

As mentioned earlier, it's best to keep sick birds in a separate cage and to place the cage in a warm, quiet place. An infra-red lamp is often used as a source of heat. Do not radiate the whole cage, but make sure that only half is radiated. If the bird's mobility is decreased, however, radiating with an infra-red light can be harmful and must be avoided. If it is too warm for the bird, it can not avoid the rays. You can also provide lukewarm chamomile tea instead of water. Chamomile tea has a soothing effect on the intestines when they are inflamed for any reason. Many diseases in birds cause non-specific signs (i.e., diarrhea or respiratory symptoms). Contact an avian veterinarian immediately if illness is suspected rather than trying to treat the condition yourself.

If the veterinarian has prescribed medications, you can give these in various ways. Always keep to the prescribed dosage. Overdosing often does more harm than good.

• Medications in liquid or powder form should be put in the drinking water or

This bird is being made to look pretty before entering a competition.

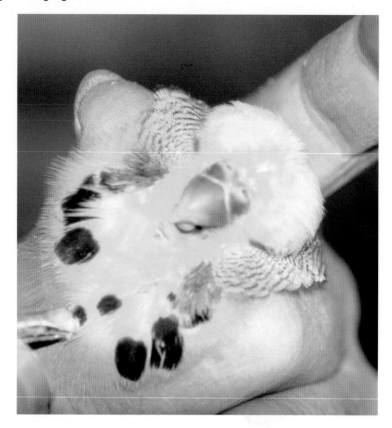

sprinkled over the seeds. Make sure that the bird has no other source of water or food, such as fruit and vegetables, at its disposal. It is possible that your bird does not think much of the taste of its drinking water or seeds with the medication. Your budgie can't know that these are good for it.

• Crush tablets and mix the powder into the food.
• If you have to give your bird the medication directly, the best way to hold a budgie tight is as follows. Hold the budgie not too tightly in one hand, bend the head back a little and pour the prescribed amount of medication into the beak, next to the tongue. The budgie will now have to swallow it. This way you will always know that the bird has had its medication.

parakeets budgerigar

Tips for the budgerigar

- Buy your budgie from a good pet store or reputable dealer.
- Pay attention to indications for health and hygiene when buying a budgie.
- Always keep new or strange birds apart from your own birds for several weeks to avoid infection.
- Never give your birds more food per day than necessary.
- Ensure that there are enough sprouted seeds and supplemented feed during the molting and brooding period.
- Budgies love millet, but they can quickly become overweight from eating it.
- Put some willow or fruit tree branches in the cage or aviary that your birds can gnaw on.

- Make sure your budgies are not in a draft and that they are free from frost in the winter.
- Good hygiene, housing, food and care can prevent many bird diseases.
- Budgies are really sociable birds. So do not keep a bird alone if you have little time for it. But overpopulation of an aviary is also not good.
- Make sure your budgie(s) have something to do when you are away. They love all kinds of games.
- Devote a lot of attention to your budgie if you want to teach it to talk.
- Budgies that are sick or brooding need quiet surroundings.

Facts on the web

American Budgerigar Society
www.aviarybirds.com/abs.htm
The official site of the American Budgerigar Society. Filled with important information for the Budgie owner.

Bird Food Quiz
www.parrothouse.com/quiz.html
A wide-ranging question-and-answer site of feeding questions and myths and other subjects regarding the care of budgies.

Toolady.com
www.toolady.com
A non-profit organization that is a great resource for all things parrot, including message boards, classified ads, information, tips, and more.

Parrot-parrot
www.parrotparrot.com
A site dedicated to lovebirds, budgies, and parrots. Filled with a wide range of avian-related topics.

Bird Hotline|Vet Talk: Your Questions Answered
www.birdhotline.com/vet.htm
Important emergency health information provided by certified avian veterinarians.

parakeets budgerigar

Breed association

American Budgeriger Society
www.aviarybirds.com/abs.htm
1704 Kangaroo
Kileen, TX 76541
(817) 699-3965

Profile of the budgerigar

Name in English:	Budgerigar (popular name budgie)
Name in Latin:	*Melopsittacus undulatus*
Origin:	Australia, especially the red hart and not in the coastal areas
Biotope:	Steppe and savanna ranges in the neighborhood of fresh water
Height:	6.3" - 7.1"
Tail length:	3.1" - 3.5"
Weight:	1.0 ozs - 1.4 ozs
Life expectancy:	In captivity: 12 to 14 years
Biorythm:	Day active
Social environment:	In pairs or in a group
Special characteristics:	Capability to learn speak and sing melodies

parakeets budgerigar